The
Black Folks'
Little
Instruction Book

Doubleday

New York
London
Toronto
Sydney
Auckland

The Black Folks' Little Instruction Book

by
Denise L. Stinson

A MAIN STREET BOOK

PUBLISHED BY DOUBLEDAY
a division of Bantam Doubleday Dell Publishing Group, Inc.
1540 Broadway, New York, New York 10036

MAIN STREET BOOKS, DOUBLEDAY, and the portrayal of a building with a tree are trademarks of Doubleday, a division of Bantam Doubleday Dell Publishing Group, Inc.

Book design by Jennifer Ann Daddio

Library of Congress Cataloging-in-Publication Data
Stinson, Denise L.
The Black Folks' little instruction book / by Denise L. Stinson. — 1st ed.
p.   cm.
"A Main Street book"—Verso t.p.
1. Afro-Americans—Life skills guides.   2. Afro-Americans—Quotations, maxims, etc.
3. Aphorisms and apothegms.   4. Conduct of life—Quotations, maxims, etc.   I. Title.
E185.86.S77   1995
973′.0496073—dc20
94-23627
CIP

ISBN 0-385-47623-X
Copyright © 1995 by Denise L. Stinson
February 1995
First Edition
4 6 8 10 9 7 5 3

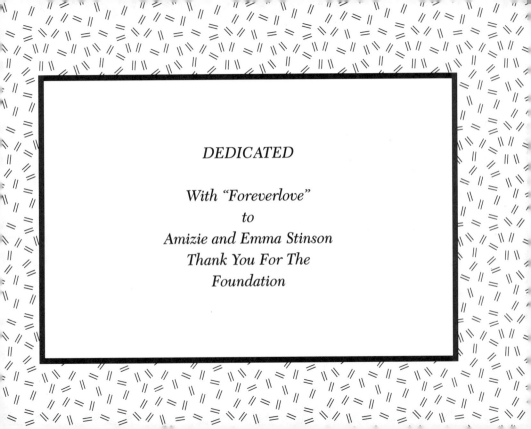

DEDICATED

With "Foreverlove"
to
Amizie and Emma Stinson
Thank You For The
Foundation

Acknowledgments

For lending their time, ideas and humor I would like to thank the following:

Freda Graham, Fred Hall, James Harvey, Yvette Jenkins, Sam Kirkland, Jojuan LaMorreia, Valerie Meyers, Fran Morgan, Michelle Morgan, Andrea Parquet, Denise Smith, Todd Taylor.

Thank you, Tsitsi Wakhisi. Your smart editing and selfless sharing of ideas once again kept me from making a complete fool out of myself. You are the best.

G. and V., you are my Buds. You will never know how much your support, faith and friendship has meant to me. I love you both.

To Diann Burns—look at us now!

Michelle Andonian, Girl, you know you make magic with that lens!

For Bruce Tracy who believed in this project when it was only a twinkle in my eye and who fought for it when it was a plank in the eyes of others. You're one of the good guys. And Martha Levin, you're just *good*!

To the agent's agent, Charlotte "Of Course You Can Do It, Honey" Sheedy, your guidance has meant the world to me.

Thank you, God, for my sister, Evelyn Bronner, the University of Michigan Journalism Fellowship Program, my WOFICC family and my wonderful life!

Introduction

Our history as African Americans has presented numerous stereotypes, challenges and reverses that have come to characterize a people. Some of the survival methods, the pains and pleasures, the coping strategies and the lessons that evolved during our social history have remained, others have been discarded.

This book is a call for us to put many of our furtive notions back on the table, while we revive some of the buried traditions, bury some of the ridiculous "righteousness" of the decades and create new thoughts.

My hope is that the *Black Folks' Little Instruction Book* will create its own perestroika, heralding an open season for open black expression. It validates worthy black traditions ("Know how to make a good sweet potato pie") while urging black people to stay abreast of the ever-evolving socio-political climate in which we live ("Read *The Autobiography of Malcolm X*"). Brothers and Sisters: it is not only *OK*, but it is *good* to think out loud about the way we live and think as African Americans in America.

This book celebrates us and all that makes us identifiable to one another. It embraces our ideals, our mannerisms, our peculiarities and our uniqueness with love and respect for the traditions that established it all. It reminds us of the good and glorious, the sad and shameful, the sordid yet savory, while reinforcing the reality that all cultures and ethnic groups enjoy the positive images and shun the negative blankets that actually cover the real identities and characteristics of personhood.

The Black Folks' Little Instruction Book, much like its published counterparts, are snippets of the day-to-day thinking in which many of us engage. And, no, it is not objective. It couldn't be. There are far too many barriers built by American society and by the people who comprise it for there to be a consensus on any one given issue. The goal of *The Black Folks' Little Instruction Book* is not about consensus-building, it is rather a twentieth-century acknowledgment of the possibilities—the ones that will make us as African Americans remember, cherish, ponder, smile!

The
Black Folks'
Little
Instruction Book

1.

Know how to bake a good sweet potato pie.

2.

Take off work on Martin Luther King, Jr.'s birthday. If it were not for him, you probably would not have that job.

3.

Take lots of pictures at family reunions.

4.

You wear reds and yellows beautifully.

5.

Be a Big Brother or Big Sister
even if you have children.

6.

Call or visit your grandparents often.

7.

Read *The Autobiography of Malcolm X.*

8.

Eat greens every chance you get.
They are full of memories and vitamin C.

9.

Start the way you can hold out.

10.
Be friends with your neighbors.
Strong communities are built one house at a time.

11.
Contribute to the United Negro College Fund.

12.
Know what Kwanzaa is.

13.
Speak to one another as you pass on the street.

14.
Don't stare at black people who choose to wear green or blue contact lenses no matter how weird you think they look. Those are their eyes, not yours.

15.
Everyone who wears dreadlocks
is not a Rastafarian.

16.
Read stories to your children with heroes and
heroines that look just like them.

17.
Every once in a while cook a good pot of beans.

18.

Don't let anyone tell you who your leaders are.

19.

Never put more than ten barrettes in your daughter's hair at one time.

20.

It doesn't matter how pretty your legs are, being ashy will make them ugly. Always use a good lotion after a bath or shower.

21.
Sweep the sidewalk in front of your house.

22.
Do not give a child a name that has more than eighteen letters to it.

23.
Be a supporting member of the NAACP.

24.

Choose your role models carefully.

25.

No one has appointed you chief of the Black Police. You have no right to judge who is black enough and who isn't.

26.

Tell your daughters they are beautiful and your sons they are handsome.

27.
Attend a church picnic.

28.
If you walk to get exercise,
try going around your block a few times.
It's a good way to meet neighbors.

29.
Don't let the Colonel, Church's or Popeye's make
you think that you don't know how to fry chicken.

30.
We are prone to hypertension.
Cut down on your salt.

31.
Remember, there is no such thing as "good" hair.
If it is yours, it's good.

32.
Like Rosa Parks, ride buses and other public
transportation with pride and dignity.

33.
Do not add *ed* to words that already end in *ed*.

34.
Construct a family tree.

35.
Sit on a front porch every chance you get.

36.
Eat more fresh fruit.

37.
Every year make a big production in your house
on the first day of school. It sets a positive tone
for the year.

38.

Support black businesses but only if you get good
service. And if you don't tell them the problem,
then give them a second chance.

39.

Don't spend more than $40 for a
pair of gym shoes.

40.

Don't be ashamed to be seen looking out of your window. There is nothing wrong with wanting to know what is happening on your street.

41.

Never talk about someone's mother.

42.

Own a Sunday hat.

43.
See *Roots*.

44.
Keep subscriptions to *Ebony, Jet* and other black periodicals.

45.
Don't believe everything you hear about Africa. Go see for yourself.

46.
Know that Jesse Jackson and Reggie Jackson
are not related.

47.
Sing gospel music.

48.
Parents, check your children's homework.

49.

Listen to jazz. It's our contribution to American music.

50.

Learn to do The Bus Stop. It will be back again.

51.

Don't be ashamed to admit that you like chitlins.

52.
Kool-Aid is still cool—but it is no substitute for water.

53.
Pray for other people.

54.
Africa is not a country.

55.
Nappy hair is a blessing.

56.
Wash your windows with vinegar and water.

57.
Know all the verses to
"Lift Every Voice and Sing."

58.
Next time the sistuh/friends get together,
do "Little Sally Walker."

59.
Stay away from cinnamon-colored panty hose.

60.
Say no to Nadinola.

61.
No matter how little Vaseline you put on your legs, they *still* look like patent leather.

62.
Love your lips.

63.
If a black business or entrepreneur disappoints you, fault that business or person, not all black businesses.

64.
CP Time is not an acceptable excuse for lateness.
Be prompt.

65.
Know that the blues ain't always sad.

66.
Have a Billie Holiday album in your house.

67.
Not every black man or youth plays or
enjoys basketball.

68.
Watermelon is not a forbidden fruit. Do not let
your enjoyment of it become a cultural dilemma.

69.
Your ancestors were enslaved men and women.
It is too simple to call them just slaves.

70.

Make a special effort to view special African and African American art and science exhibits.

71.

Respect your elders no matter how old you get.

72.

Don't let your fear of racism keep you from following your dreams.

73.

When times get tough, rejoice in the knowledge
that you are one in a long line of proud,
courageous people who have a history
of surviving.

74.

Join an investment club.

75.

Specific and Pacific are not the same thing.

76.
Organize a Sojourner Truth tea.

77.
Never conversate.

78.
Coffee does not make you black.

79.
Learn to cornrow.

80.
Never use a corn bread mix.

81.
Never stop dreaming of a better life.

82.
Be happy about your big hips and thighs.

83.
It's OK to scratch your head,
even if it doesn't itch.

84.
If you are thinking about making a career change,
consider teaching.

85.
Take your extensions *down*
before they take you down.

86.
If you get the chance, own an old pink Cadillac.

87.
Your kids will have a number of friends
throughout their lives but only one mother and
father. Have the courage to be a parent.

88.

Hold hands every chance you get.

89.

If you give a party, play a lot of Motown music.

90.

There may be times in your life when you need more help than your friends and family can provide. Love yourself and see a therapist.

91.

Racism and sexism are partners in crime.
Don't be afraid to call them both out.

92.

Don't be so important and distant in your
corporate job that you can't have a genuine
conversation with those who do custodial work
in the building.

93.
Learn how and when to back down
in an argument.

94.
If you're not having fun dancing,
you're probably trying to impress people.

95.
Invite friends and family to a
Crispus Attucks picnic.

96.
Take the time to spend some time alone.

97.
Measure your success only by what you want out of life, not by what other people tell you you should have.

98.
Always tell the truth. Few things are more discouraging than realizing you have just lied on your lie.

99.
Support black films and theater.

100.
Don't wait for opportunities, make them.

101.

Be a mentor. Sharing your experience
and knowledge is one of the greatest gifts
you can give.

102.

Learn to disagree without disrespecting.

103.

When someone does something nice for you,
take a moment to write them a thank you note.

104.
You are never too old to improve yourself.
Don't be afraid to go back to school.

105.
Volunteer at a neighborhood community center.

106.
Be fair with one another.

107.
If you are a supervisor of white employees,
don't make special privileges for them
just so they will like you.

108.
Encourage your children to write.
We need chroniclers of all of our experiences.

109.
Never use frozen collard greens.

110.
Make biscuits on Sunday mornings.

111.
Calling someone "High Yellow" or "Red Bone"
is not a compliment.

112.
Save your grandmother's quilts.

113.
Greyhound buses and fried chicken go together
like a hand and glove.

114.
If you can eat more than one meal from your
"plate to take home," you are taking too much.

115.
If there is not a line for the barber's chair,
find another barber.

116.
Don't do inferior work for a black boss,
teacher or professor.

117.
The Civil War was not only about us.

118.
All bald black men do not look like Lou Gossett.

119.
There is too much black history to fit into the month of February. Keep learning.

120.
Abraham Lincoln had an ulterior motive.

121.
Savings accounts, not lotto numbers, make dreams come true.

122.

Real prophets don't advertise in newspapers or have 900 numbers.

123.

There are no such things as illegitimate children, there are only illegitimate parents.

124.

If your earrings can double as hoola hoops, they're too big.

125.
The great equalizer is a sharp mind
not a loaded gun.

126.
If you can sit on your hair,
your extensions are too long.

127.
Pinching a baby's nose will not make it keen.

128.
Your gym shoes should not have more features than your car.

129.
There was a time when all we had was our word. Honor that.

130.
To have a job is a privilege. Always do your best.

131.
Of course you deserve it, but can you afford it?

132.
Listen to all sides of an argument before making up your mind about who is right or wrong.

133.
A sense of respect for others and for themselves is one of the best presents you can give your children.

134.
One of the greatest gifts you can give yourself
is forgiveness.

135.
Make a date with your sweetheart to watch
the sunset.

136.
Take a black studies course.

137.
If you do not want to get a baby-sitter,
only go to the early movie.

138.
Be known as an encourager not a discourager.

139.
Take good care of old pictures.

140.
Real class can never be bought or sold.

141.
When someone tells you they do not want to
discuss something at that time, leave it alone.

142.
Give massages.

143.
Make your bed every day.

144.
Never date a man with his initials carved in
his hair.

145.
Never date a man who spends more time at the
beauty parlor than you.

146.

Just because you know the truth doesn't mean that everyone wants to hear it. Use discretion.

147.

Never wear a hairdo that requires you to sleep sitting up.

148.

Develop "The Look" our parents and grandparents had instead of the slap.

149.
Clothes are not a long-term investment.

150.
Don't expect your hair to look like the picture and you won't be disappointed.

151.
Don't say anything bad about anyone whose last name is Washington, you could be related to them.

152.
Gym shoes shouldn't come with an
owner's manual.

153.
You shouldn't need a Friend of the Court to
introduce you to your children.

154.
Don't let mixing Magic Shave become a lost art.

155.
BLACK BOTTLED-BLONDES:
Yeah, sure, only your hairdresser knows!

156.
You have to be a friend to have a friend.

157.
Try African dance as an aerobic exercise.

158.
It's OK to set your purse on the floor
if that's where you want to put it.

159.
Learn how to cut the kernels off fresh corn.

160.
Own a rocking chair.

161.
Never brush your hair while it is still wet.

162.
Forget about your hair. Learn to swim!

163.
Be careful not to quit a job in anger.

164.
Don't yell, "Hey you!" It's rude.

165.
Keep in touch with the people you liked in school.

166.
Tell one another stories. We are a people
from a long and great oral tradition.

167.
Sit in the front of the church.

168.
Have frequent conversations with God.

169.
Never do anything you wouldn't want your
children to know about.

170.
Introduce your children by name. They are more
than just your son or your daughter.

171.
If the opportunity is there,
build an extended family.

172.
One of the greatest gifts you can give your children is to let them see you tell the truth when lying would be much easier.

173.
Every now and then take a little time for yourself. It will help you be a better father/mother/sister/brother/wife/husband/friend.

174.
People are happiest when they feel useful.
Make routine household chores a family affair.

175.
Give birthday parties and serve homemade cakes.

176.
Know the parents of your children's friends.

177.
Learn CPR.

178.
Have a hobby.

179.
Recycle.

180.

Surround yourself with people who feel good about themselves.

181.

Write fairy tales for your children that feature black characters.

182.

Never let a man come between you and your Sistuh/friend.

183.
Respect the feelings and opinions of children.

184.
Buy art by black artists.

185.
Tour a historic Underground Railroad site.

186.
If you do not take control of the situation, the situation will invariably take control of you.

187.
Remember that praise is more fun than criticism.

188.
Learn to respect other people's privacy.

189.
Identify the things that you do well and
learn to do them better.

190.
Organize a block club.

191.

As a community, we cannot complain about our children's substandard education if we do not become involved in the system. Attend school board and PTA meetings and let them know what you think.

192.

Reading is a privilege that we were once denied. Join a reading club.

193.
Don't be stingy with your I love you's.

194.
Give second chances.

195.
Take a youngster to work with you so that he or she can see what you do.

196.
Black sheep have the finest wool.

197.
Dream of a black Christmas.

198.
Compliment a Sistuh.

199.
Not having a lot of money is no excuse not to read. Get library cards for you and your children.

200.
Being black does not exempt you from skin cancer. Use sunscreen.

201.
Double Dutch is a fine art.

202.
Offer African folk tales in addition to
Mother Goose at storytime.

203.
Acknowledge our black sheroes.

204.
Have a Juneteenth picnic.

205.
Behind a basketball is not the only way our young men should know how to fly.

206.
S K A T E !!!!

207.
It's OK to encourage your children to color faces in a coloring book different shades of brown.

208.
Send black greeting cards.

209.
Use a little kente cloth in your outfits.

210.
Black women are tired of being described as sassy.

211.
There's a black side to Europe.
Don't discount it as a vacation choice.

212.
We are a diaspora. We may not all sound alike or
call the same place home but as black people we
share more than we realize.

213.
When your children are young, treat them the
way you want them to treat you when you are old.

214.
Keep alive the Southern tradition of planting or
putting out flowers every spring.

215.
Look people in the eye when
you shake their hand.

216.
Admit when you are wrong.

217.
If the topic of the conversation only focuses on what the "man" has done to us, we'll never get around to talking about what we can do for ourselves.

218.
Take a firm stand against drugs in your home
and your community.

219.
Be leery of restaurants that boast of serving
the biggest ham hocks and the best pizza
on the same menu.

220.

Learn how to sew and how to type.
You will always be able to make extra money.

221.

Never argue with the police.
Take your complaint to a court of law.

222.

Firearms are not toys. If you must have them,
teach everyone in your home to respect them.

223.
Make a will even if you don't think you have anything to leave anyone.

224.
Decide what type of language and behavior is acceptable in your home and make this information known to those who visit.

225.

You have a right to understand anything that you are asked to sign. Take your time, read it and question anything you don't understand.

226.

Monitor the images your children are exposed to on television for those that tell them that as people of color they are not beautiful, desirable, smart or good.

227.
Never tell your friends how much money
you make.

228.
Learn how to make a pie crust from scratch.

229.
Always use fresh fruit in your cobblers.

230.
Use corn bread rather than white bread
for your dressing.

231.
Every now and then shout "Amen" during a good
church sermon. Preachers like that!

232.
Invite your pastor and his wife over for dinner.

233.
Volunteer to do work in your church.

234.
Don't be wishy-washy.
Let your yes be yes and your no be no.

235.
Fear and doubt work together to paralyze you.
Courage and hope work together to
move you forward.

236.
Don't trust people who start sentences with "Trust me."

237.
Don't play Bid Whist with people who can't take a joke.

238.
Always leave a key on the inside of a deadbolt lock.

239.
Be bold. Ask for what you want and don't be afraid to work hard to get it.

240.
Learn three new words each week.

241.
Make tea cakes for your kids.

242.
Be loyal to your friends and family.

243.
Help keep your communities clean. Don't litter.

244.
If you live in a state that pays for bottle and can return, leave them in a plastic bag outside for the homeless.

245.
Don't allow yourself to be lumped with other people simply because you share the same-color skin. Embrace your uniqueness.

246.
If you are an eyewitness to a crime, tell the police what you know.

247.

If your children have to do a report on an American president or national figure, help them research that person's track record with the African American community of that time.

248.

Keep African traditions alive at wedding ceremonies. Jump the broom or invite live drummers!

249.
Support and visit black history museums.

250.
Children need to come of age through tradition
not trial and error. Investigate your area's
offerings of rites of passage programs.

251.

If you have to leave your neighborhood for a haircut, your local black newspaper, church or collard greens, you should rethink calling your neighborhood your community.

252.

Apologize to no one if you include Western operas, ballets and classical music among your entertainment experiences.

253.
Don't let Betty Crocker make you doubt
your pound cake.

254.
Bend over backward to make it to all of
your family reunions.

255.
Black women, stand in front of the mirror as long as it takes you to accept and appreciate your natural beauty.

256.
Learn how to give a pedicure.

257.
Neither be too arrogant nor too ignorant to use food coupons at the grocery store.

258.

Question anyone who wants to be your leader, black or white.

259.

When planning a vacation, investigate the black history of the area.

260.

Plan a Booker T. Washington dinner.

261.
Don't gloat if you become the "first" black in your position. It's really more of a shame that it has taken so long.

262.
Learn another language.

263.
Report child abuse. It's everybody's business.

264.
Don't take for granted that your mother or your grandmother will raise your children.

265.
If you are a workaholic, think of your spouse and children as part of your job description.

266.
Don't love your possessions to the extent that you can't stand the thought of giving them up.

267.
Completely bury the stereotype that blacks from the South are less intelligent or sophisticated than their Northern counterparts.

268.
Support black colleges.

269.
Bring cheer to residents in black convalescent homes.

270.
When your integrated neighborhood becomes
50 percent black, don't you run, too.

271.
Mothers, don't make your oldest son serve as a
surrogate father to the rest of your children.

272.
Mothers, your oldest daughter is not
your permanent stand-in.

273.
Encourage your children to volunteer in the community before they seek their first job.

274.
Don't excuse corruption on the part of black officials with: "They're just doing what the white man does."

275.
A church choir is an excellent place to launch
a singing talent.

276.
Thank God for every day of life.

277.
Let your children see you pray.

278.
Don't pull out those disingenuous "black" excuses to get out of a jam at work or school.

279.
Begin your day with a prayer.

280.
Don't change your manner of speech to impress other people.

281.
Don't wear to bed what you have worn all day.

282.
Grocery stores and restaurants in your community
do not have a license to be less hygienic,
courteous or dependable.

283.
Eating fried chicken with your hands is
acceptable on all occasions.

284.
Try white-water rafting, lacrosse.

285.
Don't spit on the street.

286.
Don't leave or break glass bottles at
neighborhood playgrounds.

287.
Don't spend more time on the phone
than you do with your kids.

288.
Disagreements happen in all families. If you can't
get along with family members, establish a
workable détente so you at least stay in touch.

289.
Don't allow anyone to behave in an obscene or
irresponsible manner around your children.

290.
Listen to and monitor the lyrics of popular songs
that your children sing.

291.

Mother, be the best example of the type of woman your son should choose for his life mate. Father, be the best example of the type of man your daughter should choose for her life mate.

292.

Allow yourself the pleasure of daydreaming.

293.

At one time, cowry shells were used in some African countries as money.

294.

Try a little cracklin' in your corn bread.

295.

If you really want to set a romantic mood, put on some old Isaac Hayes albums.

296.
Don't barbecue after dark.
How can you tell if the food is done?

297.
Know that under the colors of our skins we are all
spirits made in the image of God, and it is the
beauty and love of our spirits that really matter.

298.
Brothers, it's OK to count your money
above the table.

299.
It is very African to stand on the corner
with your friends and socialize.

300.

Buy fresh produce from African American trucks and stands. Nine times out of ten, it's fresher and cheaper than the local supermarket's.

301.

A new outfit on Easter doesn't make you a better person. God only has eyes for your heart.

302.

For perspective, visit a neighborhood that is far better and far worse than yours.

303.

Shouting should not be the usual way you talk to people to get them to do something.

304.

Prepare a meal from a different ethnic culture.

305.
Invite your children's teacher and principal to
your home for dinner, a party or family gathering.

306.
Ask your barber if he/she washes combs after
each customer.

307.
Welcome an African exchange student
into your home.

308.
If you disagree with what someone has done to you, tell that person, not that person's friends.

309.
Hold on to your bread pudding recipes.

310.
For dating purposes, it is pretentious to ask a man on a first meeting if he has a car.

311.
For dating purposes, it is presumptuous on a first meeting to ask a woman how many children she has.

312.
For dating purposes, it is acceptable on a first meeting to ask a man who is not in school or the military if he is employed.

313.
Let your children see you reading.

314.
Make and keep dental appointments.

315.
Visit your children's classroom twice a year.

316.
Stop smoking.

317.
Don't start smoking.

318.
Know what each letter stands for in NAACP, SCLC, UNITA and UNCF.

319.
Know your family history and discover the heroes and sheroes in your own family tree.

320.
Never tell your children to put on their best behavior in the presence of white company; teach them to have their best behavior in all company.

321.
Don't leave it to chance for our children
to understand sensitive subjects that involve
black celebrities and leaders.
Explain the situations to them.

322.
Know the names, addresses and phone numbers
of the parents with whom your children associate.

323.

You can't breathe a sigh of relief just because your children's playmates are white. Children will be children, no matter the race.

324.

Patronizing currency exchanges or other check cashing institutions in our communities may be expedient, but it is not prudent.

325.
Children of separated or divorced parents should
be told about the good points and good times you
had with the departed spouse or mate.

326.
Make a point to read the Frederick Douglass
speech: "What to the Slave Is the Fourth of July?"

327.
Read some of the mystery stories written by
black authors.

328.
If your car note is more than your rent,
you should consider trading in the vehicle
for a house note.

329.
God is not only able, He is willing.

330.
The civil rights movement is not ancient history.

331.
Maintain your property.

332.
Become familiar with the struggles of other ethnic groups in the United States.

333.
Never refer to yourself as a (minor)ity.
You are major.

334.
Encourage black radio stations to do more
community news programming.

335.
Learn more about how to save and
invest your money.

336.
Write letters to the editor.

337.
Follow Malcolm X's advice: Wear a watch.

338.
Patronize black bookstores. They supported black
writers long before we were in vogue.

339.
No matter how old or far away you get, talk to your parents at least once a week.

340.
Set up a family charity or loan fund for relatives at your family reunions.

341.
Observe the movie ratings established to monitor sex, violence and inappropriate or sensitive materials for children of certain ages.

342.
When your marriage is in trouble, seek professional and pastoral help.

343.
If the fashion does not fit your form,
don't buy the outfit.

344.
Attend the Martin Luther King, Jr., Marcus
Garvey and Malcolm X community
parades and celebrations.

345.
Use black hair-care products.

346.
Buy black dolls that have African features,
not white dolls painted black.

347.
Be vocal that medical research includes
conditions that primarily affect
African Americans.

348.
Register to vote.

349.
Hand me downs are not put downs.

350.
Remember that your true source is God.